From the ICU Waiting Room

by
Theresa Schwartz, M.D.

authorHOUSE™

1663 LIBERTY DRIVE, SUITE 200
BLOOMINGTON, INDIANA 47403
(800) 839-8640
WWW.AUTHORHOUSE.COM

First published by AuthorHouse 2/10/2006

ISBN: 1-4208-6430-0 (sc)

Library of Congress Control Number: 2005905430

Printed in the United States of America
Bloomington, Indiana

This book is printed on acid-free paper.

To my Aunt, Ruth Schwartz
who showed me the reason to take life
one day at a time

Ruth Schwartz never knew a stranger. She could be counted on for anything—a shoulder to cry on, a room to sleep in, or simply a conversation over cocktails. She was always the first one to give laughs during parties and support during tragedies. Her bright red hair spoke volumes about her personality. She was always the center of attention and she would never let a crowd down. A phenomenal hostess, Aunt Ruth always had room for one more person and was full of stories to entertain her guests. Many people loved Ruth Schwartz. Many people considered her a close friend. But, only a few of us were fortunate enough to call her family.

As the fifth of seven children, Ruth found ways to make herself unique. Never one for rules or regulations, Ruth tended to do things in her own way on her own time schedule. These characteristics made her one of the most spontaneous, fun-loving people the town of Centralia, IL has ever seen. Aunt Ruth was the type of person that anyone—no matter how well you truly knew her—felt comfortable stopping by her house and swapping stories over a few drinks. She was always the first to arrive at a party and the last to leave. There wasn't a gathering in town that didn't have her on the guest list. Everyone's friend—that's one of the best ways to describe Aunt Ruth.

Aunt Ruth had no children of her own and she never dated after she lost "Doc"—her common law husband who passed away in 1993. She became a part of everyone else's family, and she was always welcomed with open arms. Aunt Ruth's immediate family—five brothers and a baby sister—always take care of each other. They grew up playing, fighting, defending and praying with one another. Regardless of the situation, nothing comes between the Schwartz's. This one-of-a-kind relationship that they share has been passed on to all of their kids and will hopefully continue through the next generation. This closeness, this respect, this unconditional love is what makes the last 37 days of my Aunt Ruth's life so remarkable.

On December 14, 2000, Aunt Ruth and her sister, my Aunt Jeannie, were heading west on Interstate 161 around 10:30 a.m. At the same time, an 18-wheeler was moving north on Route 4. Aunt Ruth's dark green Mercedes SUV met the semi at the intersection of these two roads. The driver of the 18-wheeler never saw the red light. Aunt Ruth never saw the semi as it ran the red light going nearly 50 miles per hour. As the semi broadsided the Mercedes and crushed in the driver's side door, the two moved as one unit nearly 200 feet. That moment ended the life of Ruth Schwartz, as we knew it...

I was 22 years old at the time of the accident. I was in the middle of my medical school applications—getting ready to start my first year of medical school in the fall of 2001. Aunt Ruth, my Dad's older sister, was always thoroughly interested in anything to do with the field of medicine. When the accident occurred, I realized after the first 48 hours that she was going to be in the hospital for a long period of time. I knew that I wouldn't be able to remember all of the details from each day, and Aunt Ruth was the type of person who would have wanted to know all of the details. So, I started a journal. I didn't want her to miss a thing. I wrote it as if she would someday read it from cover to cover and really understand all that had happened throughout the hospitalization. It was kind of like writing a letter to her every day. It was my way of talking to her when regular conversation wasn't possible. It was my way of connecting with her during the difficult, confusing and unstable times in the ICU waiting room…

Thursday, December 14, 2000

The accident occurred at 10:30 a.m. at the intersection of Route 161 and Route 4. Initial reports of the accident from Mascoutah Police went to Steve Schwartz. We think they saw the address as "Patriot Road" and assumed you lived in the same household.

Word of the accident went through the family chain. Dad heard the news from Mom at the Poplar Place. He left his lunch on the table and headed to the farm at 12:15 p.m. Smitty came to the accident scene before the truck was towed.

Dad, Grandma, Uncle Phil, Uncle Steve and Uncle Tom left from the farm in Dad's truck. They picked up Uncle Dave at his house and headed for St. Louis at 12:38 p.m.

Mom called me at 12:15 p.m. in Collinsville. She said a social worker at the Emergency Room at the hospital needed to meet with a family member immediately.

I arrived at the E.R. at 12:35 p.m. You hadn't been entered into the computers yet because they weren't sure of your identity. Your purse was still in the Mercedes. Two social workers brought me into the "Quiet Room"—a private room across the hall from the regular E.R. waiting room.

They told me you were in a very serious car accident and had sustained a blow to your head. You were in getting a CT scan to see what kind of damage had been done to your brain. They said the CT scan would tell them what decisions needed to be made.

You were already on a ventilator—had been since arriving at the hospital. A central line was going to be put in your shoulder to administer IV fluids. The person who tried to put the catheter in accidentally slipped it into an artery instead of a vein. This cut off some of the blood supply to the back of your brain. After the CT scan, you were sent to Interventional Radiology. They wanted to make sure your aorta was alright—they thought that the blood they were seeing pool in your neck from the catheter accident was from a ruptured aorta. I'm sure they were freaking out—considering they cut off blood to part of your brain for several minutes.

After the resident radiologist left the Quiet Room from talking to me, your brothers and Grandma showed up. An ER doctor that treated you came in to talk to all of us—me, Jessica, Dad, Grandma, Steve, Dave, Phil and Tom.

He told us that you have several broken bones: humerus, ulna, radius, pelvis and tibia. These, he said, were no big deal. The problem was with your brain. You had a subdural hematoma—a fancy name for bleeding on your brain. At this time, they didn't know what kind of brain damage you had sustained.

We all went up to the 8400 ICU waiting room and met Father Jim Doughtery at around 3:30 p.m. The nurse who would be with you for the evening came in the room to tell us you would be in the ICU as soon as you were finished in radiology.

At 6:00 p.m., I started hanging out in the hallway to figure out where you were. I walked into the unit as someone walked out and asked the secretary if you were coming up soon. Just then, you were wheeled by me on a bed.

Your face was covered in blood and you had a gash on your forehead. I went in to let the others know that you had arrived and we needed to wait on the staff to hook you up before we could visit you in your room.

Close to 7:00 p.m., we got to come in to see you in two shifts. Fr. Jim went in first to anoint you. We could only stay for a few minutes. After we saw you, a trauma surgeon and orthopedic surgeon explained what needed to be done. Everyone left the hospital around 7:30 p.m. to head home.

Around midnight, me, Corey, Dad and Jessica came back. Me and Dad stayed the night. An ICU doctor told us that a "bolt" would be put into your head to measure your intracranial pressure. With all the blood on your brain, they wanted to monitor your pressure to gauge how serious the damage was. This was done sometime between 2:00-5:15 a.m. Friday morning. As of right now, the doctors cannot say for sure that you will survive. Everything is minute to minute, and we are scared to death.

Calls: Suzanne
Stayed overnight Thursday: Tony and Theresa

Friday, December 15, 2000

Dad and I got to see you at 5:15 a.m. The bolt was already in place and your intracranial pressure was over 20—too high. Your face was <u>very </u>swollen. You had been given a ton of fluids and you were almost unrecognizable. The blood had not been removed from your face or hair. We were able to say good morning, but we couldn't stay long.

The head duck in the SICU came to talk to us in the waiting room at 6:40 a.m. He told us that your surgery for the broken bones was postponed to Monday. Since the doctors could not estimate the extent of the damage to your brain, they weren't sure you were stable enough to handle a full day of surgery. The surgery to fix your hip socket needed to be put off for 5-7 days. An injury as serious as yours tends to cause a ton of bleeding and you definitely did not need any more blood loss. They wanted to wait until your blood counts and clotting factors had increased before they tried to fix your hip.

At 10:15 a.m., Grandma, Uncle Tom and Uncle Steve arrived. At 11:00 a.m., after rounds were finished, two trauma surgeons and an orthopedic surgeon brought us back into the conference room to discuss your progress overnight. This scared us. Using no uncertain terms, the head trauma surgeon told us that they weren't sure you would live. The reasons were explained:

4

1) Possible complications from the botched catheter. Due to the cut-off artery, you had a stroke. There was some bleeding in your cerebellum, as shown by a new CT scan. They expected the damage from the stroke to continue to progress, and they couldn't predict what the bleeding would do. Dad made him explain twice how they could possibly have made this life-threatening mistake. Needless to say, he was furious.

2) Bleeding and swelling could continue in your brain. It was impossible for them to say whether or not you were done bleeding. Although the rest of your organs were working, they weren't sure that your brain would continue to work.

The orthopedic surgeon told us again that you desperately needed surgery to fix your broken bones. It would take plates, rods and screws to fix your bones, and they needed to do it as soon as possible. However, it would not be done until your brain was ready to handle it. Dad and I left at 11:15 a.m. Steve, Tom and Grandma stayed around for another hour. When we left, we weren't very confident. The pressure on your brain was over 20 mmHg, whereas in a healthy person, the pressure is 3-5 mmHg. You did not look good, due to the excessive swelling. The doctors didn't sugarcoat the possible complications that could come your way. We knew you weren't out of the woods and it was frightening.

Dr. Bruce Frank came by to check on you. He talked to Dad about how you could possibly progress. He said that you cannot estimate the extent of the damage this soon after the accident because the bleeding and inflammation usually continue for 3-5 days. Then, a plateau usually develops where you stop getting worse. Soon, you start to get better. This pattern could take days or weeks depending on the patient. Basically, he told us that we needed to wait and see how you worked with the trauma.

You were on mannitol to help shrink your cells to decrease the swelling in your brain and the rest of your body. You were also on Fentanyl—a narcotic that is 100 times stronger than morphine. It kept you knocked completely out and also kept you from being able to breathe on your own. You weren't on a feeding tube—only sugar water. Your left leg has been put in traction to keep your hip in place until they could take you to surgery. You were awful beat up.

Around 1:30 p.m., me, Dad and Corey were eating lunch at Red Lobster in Fairview Heights. Dad had not eaten a real meal since Thursday morning. On the way into the restaurant, Dad remembered that he forgot his cell phone. When he got back to the truck, it was ringing. A neurosurgeon called to say that you had opened your eyes when he reduced your sedation. This was fantastic news! We left the hospital very upset, and knowing that you opened your eyes gave us hope. Dad called everyone and let them know the good news.

Friday evening, Phil and Debbie stayed with you at the hospital. Everything remained constant overnight—no better, no worse.

Calls: Sadona, Pam
Visitors: Valerie

Saturday, December 16, 2000

Phil, Debbie and Dad were here in the early morning. Around 10:00 a.m., a neurosurgeon told them that you had wiggled your fingers and toes on command when they reduced your sedation. Great sign! Everyone was excited. Brain pressure was still 17-20, which the doctors said was acceptable. Blood pressure was still fine. Ventilator was still doing 100% of your breathing.

Mom and Vern came to see you all day. Jane Shaw, Jimmy "Bud" Schwartz, Randa and her mother all stopped by for a little while. No changes throughout the afternoon. Still on mannitol to keep the swelling in your head down and fentanyl to keep you sedated.

The neurosurgeon talked to me, J, Val, Corey, Jane and Vern. Dad and Mom had just left because there were some complications with Aunt Jeannie and they headed to St. Elizabeth's to see what they could find out. The doctor explained your stroke to us again and told us that you would probably not need surgery to remove the blood clot. Your body should dissolve it on its own. Also, when they reduced your sedation this morning, he called your name and you opened both eyes and looked for him. You also squeezed his hand. All positive happenings! He also talked about what might happen to you because of the stroke. Since the clot is in your cerebellum, you might not be able to see peripherally out of your left eye. Also, you might not have great coordination. He explained it like you were a piano—your black and white keys are working fine—you will be able to see and move. But, your floor keys might not be perfect—peripheral vision and hand coordination could be affected. You are still not out of the woods, but things are looking up.

You had a great nurse. He kept us up to date and answered all of our questions. He took good care of you—Dad even liked him!

The focus today is on getting your ICP down. Your bone surgery has been postponed again—they don't know when it will be rescheduled.

Your swelling went down tremendously. Your face was looking **much** better. They found out that your right ankle and right shin are both broken as well. They won't require surgery, but you will be in a cast.

No CT scan today—they didn't think that enough time had passed to be able to tell the difference from the one you had Friday. Since they didn't do the scan, they couldn't tell us whether the brain swelling/bleeding or blood clot had gotten any worse. We had to wait until Sunday to figure out what was going on in your head. You had a fever—they didn't know where the infection was.

Tom and Nancy stayed the night with you Saturday night. There were no changes reported throughout the night.

Visitors: Bonnie, Vern, Val, Tony, Phil, Debbie, Jane, Theresa, Jessica, Corey, Randa, Randa's mother, Jimmy

Sunday, December 17, 2000

You went down for a CT scan first thing in the morning. You had some problems as soon as you got down to the room. You are almost sitting up in your bed, and that is how you have been since they put you in the ICU room. When you got the CT scan, they had to lay you flat. You did not like that at all. Your ICP went up to 44 mmHg, when it was only 6-8 before you went down for the scan. Because of this, they only got pictures of your face and head, but they couldn't get one of your hip. They gave you another dose of mannitol to get the pressure to go down. The last shot of this was given at 11:30 a.m.

The CT scan looked good—you had not gotten any worse. But, you were still running a fever. Some doctors thought it was a natural response to the trauma, while others figured you had an infection in your lungs. Many people get pneumonia or other lung infections when they are on a ventilator. Plus, you had a chest tube and that makes you prone to infection as well. Basically, they aren't sure exactly what is causing your fever, but they have been giving you antibiotics since you got here. They will just wait and see.

You were breathing good, so they dropped the support the ventilator was giving you from 100% to 50%. You worked well with this. Also, we were told that the bolt in your head could not be removed until you had been off mannitol for 24 hours. That would be 11:30 a.m. Monday morning. They couldn't guarantee it would be removed, but it was a possibility.

By midnight, your head pressure was down to 10-13 mmHg. Your blood pressure and other vitals were good, and you looked very comfortable.

Visitors: Suzanne and Scott, Tony, Tom, Nancy, Theresa, Jessica, Corey, Val.

At 9:30 p.m., Tim and Joretta showed up from Kentucky. They checked you out and talked with us for a while about what was going on. Me and Dad stayed the night with you.

Monday, December 18, 2000

We talked to your nurse at 6:30 a.m. right before rounds started. Your ICP was ranging from

7-9 mmHg and your oxygen saturation was over 95. She said you were stable overnight, although you still had a fever. She had given you aspirin and suppositories to try and get your temperature down. When she was taking your temp this morning, she said you moved your lips—possibly trying to fight having something else put in your mouth. This is a great sign that you might be responding to some kinds of stimuli!

They are trying to get you off the blood pressure medicine. It works to keep your blood pressure up to make sure your brain is getting enough blood. You are not needing as much medicine now, according to the neurosurgeons. There is a formula that they use to determine what your blood pressure needs to be and how much medicine needs to be administered to give enough blood to your brain. Now, it looks like you don't need as much medicine to keep your b.p. up. Very encouraging!

At 11:30 a.m., we went in to see you—me, Dad, Tim and Joretta. Your ICP was down to 6-8 mmHg and you looked good. You're still getting tylenol every 4 hours to keep your fever under control.

At 12:30 p.m., a SICU fellow and SICU resident talked to me and Dad in the conference room. The fellow talked to us about where you are right now. Your surgeries could occur at any time—whenever the neurosurgeons give the go ahead. The head doctors are concerned with your brain pressure and they want to make sure you are completely ready to handle hours of surgery. The only thing he could say for sure was that you wouldn't have surgery this morning, and, since it was close to 1:00 p.m., that information didn't help us out much.

He talked about a new addition—your feeding tube. He said that nutrients in food help a person's immune response. Since you currently have a fever near 103°F, you obviously are fighting off something. The doctors just wanted to give you a boost. They still haven't pinpointed the cause of your fever. It could be any one of a number of things:

1) Fat globules from your broken bones causing an infection

2) Infected "bolt" in your head

3) Cytokine response from the trauma

4) Infection in your lungs—possibly from ventilator/chest tube

All in all, he basically told us that you are better than you were 24 hours ago. But, everything is minute to minute. As soon as the neuro team decides that you are stable, things will start to happen.

A research coordinator came in to talk to Dad at 1:00 p.m. She wanted to include you in a study that tested your reaction, while on sedation, to visual and audio stimuli. Dad wasn't sure if you would be a good subject for the study because of the possibility that the stroke affected your peripheral vision. He will talk about it with Grandma,

Jeannie and your brothers to decide what is best for you. He basically told her "No."

Dad, Father Jim and I went in to see you at 1:30 p.m. You were getting a chest X-ray. The SICU resident that we talked to in the conference room earlier was messing with you because a nurse had said you were twitching your eyelids. She couldn't get you to do it by talking to you, but me and Dad could. You twitched several times when we talked to you, but you rested calmly when we didn't. It made us feel like you could hear us.

The head ICU doctor talked to us outside of your room, and he told us that your chest x-ray did not look good. Due to broken ribs, your left lung is very bruised and swollen—which would make it difficult for you to breathe. Your right lung is also having trouble—fluid is staying in there causing you to cough. We just need to wait on your body to fix the little things before we can understand the big picture.

I saw you for the last time Monday at 5:15 p.m. Me, Corey, Phil and Debbie got to come into your room. You looked better, and your eyes were twitching when we were talking. A respiratory therapist came in and ticked you off though. He was putting a bronchodilator into your ventilator. It works like an inhaler. He shot two or three bottles of that stuff in your body and you got agitated. It made you cough to get the junk out of your lungs, and it was hard for you due to the multiple tubes stuck in your mouth. Your ICP jumped from 6-9 to 47 in a matter of seconds. Once he suctioned your lungs out, the ICP went back under 10 mmHg. You were still running a fever. Also, they wanted to remove the central line that is in your groin and put it someplace a little more comfortable for you. They tried to put it in your left shoulder (using the same method that gave you the stroke), and it didn't work. The nurse said that there was an "occlusion," and I'm not sure what that means yet. I'll find out though. But, that's why you have a patch and some bleeding on your left shoulder. There was already a lot of bruising and swelling on that shoulder from your seatbelt, so that whole area is pretty beat up.

There is a possibility that you will have a trachea tube put in soon. They want to get you off of the tube down your throat for a few reasons:

1) Difficult to breathe with it—the doctors said it was like breathing through a straw.

2) Damaging to vocal cords—the tube goes right between them and makes them very sore.

3) Increased risk of infection—in general, the tube down your throat makes it easier for you to get lung/respiratory infections.

A trach tube would make it a lot easier for you to breathe because the air doesn't have to travel through as much dead space to reach your lungs, it does not do anything to your vocal cords, and you have a smaller chance of getting a respiratory infection. We don't know when this might be done, the doctors just wanted to bring up the option.

You looked good when we left the room. Your blood pressure was up, your brain pressure was down, and you looked comfortable.

Calls: Randa, Kittie
Stayed overnight Monday: Uncle Phil and Aunt Debbie

Tuesday, December 19, 2000

I called the nurse at 9:30 a.m. She said you were fine throughout the night. The neurosurgery team might take the "bolt" out today! This is fantastic news! They might also take your collar off today—you are wearing a large brown neck brace that holds your head in place. The neurosurgeon wanted to get it off before it broke any skin and gave you any further discomfort. They are going to do some x-rays to make sure your neck would be okay on its own—without the support—and then make the final decision.

This afternoon, things started to get bad. Your fever spiked up to 105°F. The doctors determined from your chest x-ray and the bacteria cultures they took from your lungs that you have pneumonia. *Pseudomonas* (I think☺) bacteria is growing in your lungs. It is commonly found in this ICU—go figure—and the doctor was not surprised that you picked it up. The nurses gave you a bath in cold water and then put rubbing alcohol on your body. You were given ice water (1 liter) down your stomach tube to help cool you down. Ice packs were put all over your stomach and chest and underneath you. Your temperature was 106°F.

At 5:00 p.m., it had gone down to 105°F. This was encouraging because anything lower than 106°F was a good sign. But, at 5:45 p.m., it jumped back up to 106°F. This caused some alarm, so they changed all of your ice bags. I was in there with you for about an hour and you were so hot you were uncomfortable to the touch the entire time. Dad and Uncle Tom went in around 6:00 p.m. and the nurse told them that some fever is good for you. You need it to help fight the infection. It does not help you if the temp. is as high as 106, but a small fever is no cause for worry. We were still very concerned.

At 9:20 p.m., Dad talked to Uncle Tom at the hospital. The nurse had just told him that your temperature was 40°C, which I calculated to be 104°F. It is going down! This is great! Now, we wait to see what happens tomorrow...Hopefully, GOOD NEWS!

Stayed Tuesday night: Uncle Tom

Wednesday, December 20, 2000

At 7:00 a.m., Uncle Tom called to tell us that you ICP was down to 0-1 mmHg. This is great

news! You obviously don't have any more bleeding or swelling on your brain now. But, you still
had a fever of 104°F. The doctors were doing their
rounds, so we won't hear anything else until this
afternoon.

At 12:15 p.m., your temp. was down to 101°F!
You were cool to the touch and looked a ton better.
The "bolt" is reading negative numbers now, indicating that you aren't having any problems with
swelling. They took a chest x-ray this morning, as
usual, and we still don't know what the results of
that were. Your lungs sound better, so we hope you
are getting better.

For the majority of today, you will be out of
the ICU. You need to get another CT scan of your
head and hip and they want to put a central line
in your shoulder. You have to go to Interventional
Radiology to get that put in, so you will be gone
for a long time. We are <u>so</u> relieved that your fever
went down and things are looking up.

You returned from the CT scan around 5:15
p.m. Your ICP stayed low throughout the procedure, and, when they rolled you over to take
a picture of your hip, you opened your eyes! We
still haven't seen your eyes open, but I'm sure we
will soon. The drugs you are on have lowered
your blood pressure as far as they are willing to
go today, and you are tolerating it well. The bolt
in your head was removed at 5:30 p.m. and they
are considering taking that collar off, pending the
result of the CT scan.

Well, I misunderstood what was going on. At 6:30 p.m.. I was in your room and one of your orthopedic surgeons came in to talk to us. The bolt had not been removed—the neurosurgeons hadn't had the opportunity to do it yet. It was no longer attached to the machines, so it wasn't measuring anything. But, here is what is supposed to happen tomorrow.

1) Orthopedic surgeons take you to the OR around 8:30 a.m. They will fix your tibia (shin), ulna and radius (forearm), and humerus (upper arm).

2) General surgeons will come in when they (ortho surgeons) are all finished and remove your ventilator and feeding tubes from your mouth and put in a trachea tube and stomach feeding tube—you should not have any tubes in your mouth!

3) Either before or after your surgery, you will be sent up to Interventional Radiology to get a central line put in your shoulder and get the other one out of your groin.

Your fever was down around 100.4°F, according to my calculations. You looked and felt a lot healthier. They did an x-ray of your stomach, so we had to leave. They just wanted to make sure your feeding tube was in the right place. It has a silver tip on the end so it can be detected by x-ray.

At 11:15 p.m., your fever had gone up to 102.2°F, but they said it was nothing to worry about. You were very agitated—you were trying to cough and clear your throat. I had to wipe some tears away from your eyes because you were having so much trouble breathing. At one point, I leaned in and talked softly to you to help you calm down, and you spit on me! I couldn't' help but laugh out loud, and no one was in there with me to enjoy it! I knew right then that you would be coming around soon. I can't wait to tell you in person!

Now, you are resting—all doped up and ready for surgery. They gave you a pint of blood to make sure you were chock full for tomorrow. Everything appears to be running smoothly. We are very pleased that your surgery is tomorrow because it means that your brain is in good shape and you are stable. Today was a very positive day!

Stayed overnight Wednesday: Tony and Theresa

Thursday, December 21, 2000

We went in to see you at 6:30 a.m. You were resting comfortably and they were still thinking you would get taken down to surgery at 8:00 a.m. You didn't go down until 9:45 a.m.

Anne took Tony's chair at 2 p.m.

(*My Dad had a chair he always sat in at the hospital, and one time during the day when he got up to wander around, my Aunt Anne sat in it. He wrote this in the journal just to give her a hard time!*)

An orthopedic surgeon came in to tell us that everything with your bones looked good. He showed us the "after surgery" x-rays. You are full of metal plates, screws and rods. Everything is in place. This happened around 4:30 p.m.

At a few minutes before 5 p.m., me and Dad talked to the head ICU doctor in the hallway after Dad went to smoke. We were in high spirits about your surgery, and then he hit us with some bad news. Your kidneys failed in the OR. When you came back to the ICU, you were blue. They knew you were hypoxic—low oxygen to your brain. Your potassium levels shot up to over 7—which is life-threatening. The surgeons could not put your trachea tube or stomach feeding tube in because you got so unstable. You still had the ventilator and feeding tubes in your mouth. At this point, the doctor didn't think that you looked good. This is the first time that he has said anything negative. He said that what was happening was not good and you were in serious trouble.

We were allowed to go in to see you around 5:30 p.m. Grandma, Uncle Dave, Aunt Anne, Uncle Tom, Dad and I got to go in two at a time because you had so many machines in your room. You didn't look very good. This morning, you had good color and looked great. Now, your coloring is very poor and the staff is worried. You are on dialysis to help keep your potassium levels down. You were starting to make urine—very little—but you were making some. They are trying to determine what made your kidneys fail. They gave us some possibilities:

1) You shot a blood clot into your lungs—this could have cut off oxygen to your brain, making you hypoxic, explaining the blue color in your face. Your body may have shut your kidneys down because it was in distress. If they find a clot in your lungs, maybe they can fix it.

2) You couldn't get enough blood to your kidneys—this could make them shut down. If this is the case, then, as soon as your kidneys get blood, things will start to work again.

3) You could've damaged your kidneys in the wreck or during the healing process—this is unlikely because you had no symptoms before your kidneys failed.

I tried to come in to see you at 6:15 p.m., but the nurse was doing stuff in your room so I couldn't. I tried again at 7:15 p.m., but there were doctors in with you. At 7:45 p.m., we were allowed to see you. You looked horrible. Your color was grayish and you were swollen. The hemodialysis brought your potassium levels back down to normal and they were going to put you on a continuous dialysis machine that is much gentler on your body.

They aren't putting much effort into finding out what made your kidneys fail. Since the incident had already taken place, they figured they would treat your symptoms and worry less about the cause. When I left for the evening, they were going to do a VQ scan to check out your lungs for a blood clot and just watch you. All we can do is wait...

Stayed overnight Thursday: Uncle Tom

Friday, December 22, 2000

I got there this morning at 11:30 a.m. I knew the doctors would be done with their rounds and I could figure out what was happening. Still no changes—you are still in very bad shape. At 12:30 p.m., you were waiting on the hemodialysis machine. Your potassium levels were up to 4.8 and the nurse said they were working to help get you back to normal. Your CK levels—they measure protein breakdown by-products—were up to 107,000. A normal person has CK levels around 1000. This is a result of a syndrome they have determined you have—rhabdomyolysis. Your muscle cells are lysing, or bursting, and releasing free proteins in your bloodstream. These proteins are toxic and need to be cleared away by your kidneys. Unfortunately, your kidneys aren't working yet, so they are building up. Your nurse thought that your urine, before the surgery, looked indicative of rhabdomyolysis. It was tea-colored, but lab results didn't show any red blood cells, so the staff wasn't worried. This is a very serious condition. It can be caused by trauma, which you surely had a lot of, and is hard to treat. One complication that results from rhabdomyolysis is acute renal failure, which you had in the operating room. Another is malignant hyperthermia. This is not a fever—it is much, much worse. It is excessive body heat from your muscles running in overdrive. I looked up these conditions, and I will explain what I know when you are awake. I want to make sure I am on the right track before I put anything in writing. I am going to talk to one of your doctors about it by myself tomorrow and see what he tells me. I want to make sure I understand what is going on first.

At 6:30 p.m., I talked to your nurse and he told me that you have a very low chance for survival. We don't know for sure if he means hours, days, weeks or what. All I know is that I am not sure if I will see you alive again, and I am scared to death. I have cried. I have begged. I have screamed. I have prayed. I have gotten pissed. I have denied. We don't know what we would do without you, and we don't want to find out. So many people love you and need you. My heart is breaking and your condition is completely out of my control. Please fight this off and get better. Please!

Today has been devastating. I want nothing more than for you to come out of this. Until tomorrow...

Stayed overnight Friday: Uncle Phil, Mat, Uncle Steve, Aunt Linda

Saturday, December 23, 2000

At 6:30 a.m., Uncle Phil called Dad and told him some bad news. Some doctors had come in throughout the night and told Phil, Mat, Steve and Linda that your condition appeared to be deteriorating and the family needed to get here. Dad talked to one of your doctors, and she seemed to think that you were heading into liver failure and your lungs were starting to fill with fluid. We were expecting you to go soon, and the entire family was notified.

By 11:00 a.m., everyone was here. There were 50 Schwartz's and then some in the waiting room. Melody called repeatedly and Jane called once. We still knew nothing about your condition. We were waiting for a doctor to fill us in.

At 12:10 p.m., me and Dad were allowed in to see you. You looked <u>much</u> better than yesterday. Your color was better—you were no longer a purplish/gray. Your feet were still blue, but that was apparently due to the blood pressure medication—Levophed—which pulls blood away from your extremities to bring it to your jukebox. Now, you are on epinephrine. This will increase your blood pressure and still get blood to your entire body.

When Dad and I were in the room with you, Bishop Gregory came by to bless you. He absolved you of all of your sins and asked us to pray with him. We all held hands and said an "Our Father" over you. I could barely get out the words—it felt like someone was punching me in the stomach. It was like we were saying a final prayer, and it was impossible to get through without crying. I don't think there is anything that could make today any easier to handle.

You are still on the ventilator—it was working at 60%. You were starting to breathe over the machine and it was messing with your blood oxygenation. They are giving you a paralyzer so that you can't breathe on your own and will relax when on the ventilator. They need to keep you on the machine because you cannot take in enough oxygen on your own—so that's why you need the paralyzer.

You are still on dialysis, of course, but we don't know what your potassium and CK (protein breakdown products) levels are currently. A doctor is <u>supposed</u> to come in soon and fill us in on what your body is doing.

Another thing—somehow your body managed to reduce your temperature. You went from 40+ to 37°C, which is normal. The malignant hyperthermia is usually fatal, but it appears to have faded for the time being. The doctors also think your muscle degradation may have slowed. But, to be honest, we don't know anything. We are very worried and very scared. We just need to wait on the doctors to tell us what you are doing.

At 4:30 p.m., the doctors were finally ready to talk to us. The whole team of trauma surgeons got together. We had talked to most of them before. Your problems are more complicated than we originally thought. Apparently, the rhabdomyolysis affected your heart by breaking down cardiac muscle. This is making it difficult for you to keep your blood pressure up high enough to get blood to your whole body. They are giving you epinephrine to keep your BP up until you can do it yourself. They told us that within 24-48 hours they will be able to tell if you are getting better or if you are on your way down. They told us we should be fully prepared for you to die. Everyone is extremely upset and confused. You mean so much to us all and we didn't want to hear this news. They said you had a 25% chance of surviving. It was very hard to hear.

I went in at 7:30 p.m. to talk to you. Your nurse was very supportive all day with all of your visitors. She answered all of our questions and told us you were in her prayers. Your next nurse was great, too. She let me hold your hand and talk to you. I asked her a lot of questions about what it would take for you to get better. She was <u>very</u> positive, and she told me not to give up hope. She thinks you can do this and we should wait and see. I am with her—I am going to continue to wait for you to fix yourself.

Your potassium levels appear to be stable, which is indicative of a stoppage of the rhabdomyolysis. You did not need the hemodialysis machine all day because you may have possibly stopped degrading your muscle cells (you have already lost at least 10%). This is great because the potassium levels won't mess with your heart. Now, you can be on the continuous dialysis machine all the time to help clean out the protein breakdown products. This will help to get your kidneys functioning again. In addition, these bad protein products are drawing calcium out of your circulation. There are phosphate groups on these by-products and they attract calcium. This is also compromising your heart function by not helping to increase your blood pressure. You are currently getting calcium through an IV to make up for what you are losing. If you can get your blood cleaned up, <u>a lot</u> of good things can happen. We need you to have strong enough heart functioning to lower the epinephrine. Time will tell...

Right before midnight, I called your nurse to see how you were doing. She was so glad to hear from me because you were doing better. The doctors were checking out your heart function, and you were doing more on your own than before. They were very pleased and they think you might have turned a corner! It looks like you are still fighting hard and that's all we can ask of you! I'll see you in the morning...

Stayed overnight Saturday: Tony and Bonnie

Sunday, December 24, 2000

At a little after 6:00 a.m., Dad talked to your nurse. She said that they just got your blood work back. Your CK levels dropped from 150,000 yesterday to 90,000 this morning. This is fantastic! She also said your heart was still going—all night, she was just monitoring you and lowering the adrenaline dosage. You appear to be doing great. He couldn't go back to see you right before rounds because they were doing some tests, but our favorite nurse is taking care of you today and he came out and gave Dad a "thumbs up" with a smile. Everything looks encouraging!

I saw you at 11:20 a.m. Your nurse was impressed with your progress. Yesterday, you were getting 30 mg/min of epinephrine. This morning, you only needed 6 mg/min to keep your blood pressure up. This was something the head doctor told us to look for as a sign of improvement. Also, they reduced the breaths per minute that the ventilator was giving you. It went from 28 to 24, and you were handling it wonderfully. They want to bring it as far down as you will let them. Since you are still on the fentanyl, you can't breathe completely on your own no matter what. You will need assistance as long as you are sedated. But, it looks like your lungs are functioning better with less effort from the machines. Great news!

Your potassium levels dropped below normal, so it definitely looks like the rhabdomyolysis has stopped. But, they had to start giving you potassium because yours got too low. Go figure!

You are still getting calcium and insulin, and you are packed full of other fluids (needed to get the drugs in your system) and you are on the continuous dialysis machine. Your temperature is lower than normal because of all of the fluids—so now they have a heating blanket on you. Just treating any problem as it arises.

You had relatively few changes throughout the day—which is fantastic. Your nurse did wash your hair though. You blinked your eyes at her while she was washing. You probably felt better—there was still blood, dirt and maybe glass in your hair from the accident.

At midnight, I talked to your new nurse. She said that everything had stayed pretty constant, except that they were going to switch your epinephrine for levophed. You no longer needed such a potent medicine to keep your heart working properly. We went to bed feeling more comfortable than we have in days!

Stayed overnight Sunday: Uncle Phil and Aunt Debbie

Monday, December 25, 2000

You had a very stable Christmas morning. We are ecstatic that we get to spend this day watching you improve. The progress you have made is the best Christmas present anyone could ask for.

Your blood CPK levels were measured at midnight and they have dropped from 90,000 to 60,000! The dialysis machine is doing its job! You are off of epinephrine, and are only requiring 4 mg/min of Levophed to keep your blood pressure up. Your nurse thinks you could do it on your own, but it doesn't hurt anything to give you this small amount to just be sure your BP is high enough. All of your vitals look good, and you appear to be in control. Once your kidneys start to work, you'll be in business! They gave you Lasix early this morning to see if they could stimulate your kidneys, but it didn't work. You always have worked on your own schedule, so we'll just wait until you are ready to start your kidneys again. You never did do things when you were instructed to!

At noon, they measured your CPK levels again. They dropped from 60,000 to 38,000. You just keep on impressing us. You look more and more like yourself than you have since the accident. What a difference a few days can make!

We talked to the new attending SICU physician. He is something else. Dad and I were pretty irritated. He likes himself—A LOT! More about him later, I'm sure. But, he did tell us that your progress will be very incremental now. You will take small steps toward getting better and you are very, very sick. We have no problem with small steps. They are also going to try to wake you up pretty soon. They took you off Ativan (I didn't know, but they started you on it Saturday) to help get you off the sedation. They want to see what you can do. We are excited about this!

Another thing—your BP is great, but they are going to continue with the levophed because they want it to stay high. This way, your kidneys and brain are thoroughly perfused with blood and, hopefully, your kidneys will kick in.

Today was a rest day for you—an opportunity for you to get more stable. We are cautiously optimistic, but we believe in our hearts that you are going to get better. We know there is a long road ahead of you, and there are a lot of people who want to help you down that road. Right now, we are concentrating on the baby steps you are taking. What a Christmas present!

So, now that you're doing better—Aunt Jeannie just got put into the hospital! She apparently has a huge blood clot in her left leg and they need to put her on blood thinners and see how bad it is. This just lets you know how bad that wreck was! Hopefully, once they get her on the right drugs the blood clot will be gone and she won't have to worry about it anymore!

Stayed overnight Monday: Theresa and Jessica

Tuesday, December 26, 2000

You had a little trouble this morning. Your nurse came into the waiting room at 3:30 a.m. and told us that your dialysis machine broke. Your blood clotted inside the machine and cracked something. You lost about 500 cc of blood on the floor and, of course, he took you off dialysis. Since you were low on blood and no longer getting fluids from the dialysis, your blood pressure went down a little—so they upped your levophed dosage to 7 mg/min. This isn't a big deal because everything will get back to "normal" once you are on dialysis again.

At 9:00 a.m., your nurse told me some good news. She had to turn you to change the pads you were laying on and clean your back and you didn't go crazy! Your oxygen percentages went down to the low 90s, but you usually get really agitated when they move you. This is a good sign that you may be getting more stable. Your lungs are still messed up from the accident, so it is no surprise that you have difficulty breathing when your body is shifted. The fact that you didn't go haywire when moved is very encouraging. Your electrolyte levels are all stable and you seem to be holding your own. The dialysis wasn't hooked up yet, but it was on its way.

Your CPK levels after midnight were down to 26,000—-you are getting closer and closer to "normal." At 11:15 a.m., your nurse told me she would measure your levels again sometime this afternoon to see how it's coming along.

At 4:00 p.m., we learned that you had been a busy girl this afternoon. I don't know if I told you before, but you have a Swan catheter in your neck to measure how well you are pumping blood throughout your body. For the last few days, you have been doing fantastic and they are going to take it out today. We love hearing that you don't <u>need</u> things. You will get a central line put into your neck or groin—I think neck.

They are also going to do a bronchoscopy on your right lung. This is where they put a big tube down into your lung and suck out all the junk to help rid your lung of excess fluid. They had to give you a small dose of paralyzer to make sure you could tolerate having a tube tickle your lung. This should help you breathe a lot better and reduce the chances of you getting an infection.

Your CPK levels were measured around 4:30—you are down to 11,500! You're doing good Foofie! We are so proud of your progress!

I called your nurse last night at 9:30 p.m. She said you were doing well. They dropped your levophed down to 1.2 mg/min! She said that she was going to get you off of it by the end of the night!

Your breathing has gotten better, but you scared the hell out of Valerie this afternoon right after they cleared your lungs out. Your head had been turned to the side when they were putting the IV in your neck. You were obviously pretty irritated, and your eyes popped open! Val threw a fit! ☺ You didn't look around—you looked straight forward for about 5 minutes. The nurse kept telling you that you had been in an accident and you were in the hospital, but you didn't respond. We think you are still stoned! ☺ But what an experience for Val! She was about to throw up!

Hopefully tomorrow will be better than today!

Wednesday, December 27, 2000

Today was a great day! During the night, your nurse was able to take you off blood pressure medication completely! You can keep your mean arterial BP up in the 70s-80s range without drugs now, and that is a huge step. You can perfuse your kidneys on your own and hopefully they will kick on!

Your kidney enzymes and whatever else they use to measure your kidney function are in the normal range. Your CPK levels are down to 6000! They really think that your CPK levels need to get down to 100 before your kidneys will work effectively. You are making 30-40 cc of urine every 12 hours. If you can start making this much every hour, then they will assume your kidneys are turned on.

They were also able to take you off the bicarbonate drip this afternoon. You were on it because you were acidotic, meaning that the pH in your body was lower than normal. Now, you are no longer acidotic and you are getting oxygen where it needs to go.

They also took you off insulin. Your pancreas appears to be working better so they don't need to administer insulin to keep your glucose in check. This is another great sign. We like removing medications!

An EKG was taken because of your high troponin levels a few days ago. We will know the results tomorrow because they didn't do it until late. They don't expect to have any problems but it needs to be done to make sure your heart is in good shape.

Throughout the night, the dialysis machine pulled off more fluid than it is supposed to—this is apparently very common. So, you got a little "dry" as they called it, and they gave you some more fluids to make up for it. This was the only problem you had all day.

We are waiting on you to wake up soon. Your fentanyl has been dropped to 100 mg. This is low enough to not make you sleep all day, so you are going to start to come to. You opened your eyes for Dad this morning. You only looked straight ahead, but that is normal. It takes a while to come out of the funk you have been living in for the past two weeks. But, we are looking forward to talking to you!

They are going to put the trachea tube and stomach feeding tube in soon. You need to be a little "more stable"—whatever the hell that means, before they will take you down to the OR again. But, that's the next big event for you! More news tomorrow...

Visitors: Jack, Connie and Jessica and Cliff, Bruce Frank, Kelly, Pastor Gullen

Stayed overnight Wednesday: Uncle Phil and Aunt Debbie

Thursday, December 28, 2000

You broke another dialysis machine! I don't know the details yet, but another machine quit on you. I don't think you leaked blood all over the place this time though ☺ Other than this, the early morning was uneventful.

Today was a slow, resting day for you. They didn't tinker with you very much, but you are still trying to wake up. Uncle Phil saw you open your eyes, but you are still gazing into space. We need to give you more time for the drugs to wear off.

Dr. Frank came back today and got to go into your room. We are hoping that he could talk to the ICU doctor and then relay the new details, but I'm not sure if he got to talk to anyone.

I talked to your night nurse around 9:30 p.m. to get the details of the day. The nurse I talked to this morning wasn't really pleasant, so I wanted to wait until the next shift started to get the scoop. You had another bronchoscopy on your right lung today because there was a "mucus plug"—whatever that is! ☺ When they did this, they had to sedate you pretty heavily and your blood pressure dropped quite a bit. They just gave you extra fluid to pump you back up. Once they dropped the sedation after the bronchoscopy was over, your BP went back to where it was before. You handled it all by yourself!

You are only on 100 mg/hr of fentanyl, dialysis, a ventilator and a feeding tube. It sounds like a lot, but it is not compared to what you were on before!

Since things are looking up, you have surgery tentatively scheduled for Tuesday. They want to fix your hip, put in your trach and feeding tube. It would be great for you to get your hip fixed and all of that stuff out of your mouth. When you wake up, things would be a lot easier for you to handle if your body was "fixed" and your mouth was empty. One nurse told me that patients with head trauma tend to wake up aggressive and even violent, so it would help matters a lot if everything was in place before you wake up for extended periods of time.

Things are going to move slowly now—you will make small steps forward, so it won't seem like you are making much progress from day to day like you have been. The doctor said that we will be able to see "big" changes, relatively speaking, from week to week now. You're doing good!

Stayed overnight Thursday: Uncle Tom

Friday, December 29, 2000

You had a different nurse for the first time today. When I talked to her this morning, she couldn't give me too much information. She only knew what had happened since her shift started at 7:00 a.m. But she did say that you are breathing on your own! They turned the ventilator off, so that any breaths you are getting, you are taking them without full assistance. The only thing the ventilator is doing is giving you CPAP—continuous positive airway pressure—to keep your lungs and alveoli open to help you out. You are inhaling and exhaling on your own! This also means that you are starting to come off of the drugs since you can breathe. The large dose of Fentanyl you were on wouldn't let you breathe alone if you wanted to. We like seeing you do things on your own. This news is very encouraging. We just want to see your kidneys get started now! But, we are thrilled to death about your lungs working. We didn't think that would happen for a long time! Way to go!

Alright—that last paragraph is a classic example of why you should not trust what a new nurse tells you over the phone without talking to a doctor first. You aren't breathing on your own. You are still on 100% life support. However, you are <u>initiating</u> every breath and that is a good sign. I will just remember to check what the nurses say <u>before</u> I put it in writing next time!

Other than that, they didn't mess with you today. The doctors just want you to rest and get as strong as possible for Tuesday's surgery. You had a good night and your doctor seems to think that the worst is over. Everything looks good!

Saturday, December 30, 2000

Today was a good day for you. The doctors were able to continue to take fluid off of you with the dialysis machine. You tolerated it very well. Your blood pressure stayed up and you looked wonderful. They were also lowering the amount of fluid you were getting through the IV. They hope to get you off the extra fluids completely.

You started to run a fever this afternoon—around 39°C. Figuring that you were fighting an infection, cultures were taken from various parts of your body. This can take up to 72 hours to figure out what bacteria are hanging out in your body. The nurses and doctors told us several days ago that you could very easily pick up an infection, so, if you had one, it wouldn't be a surprise. They just want to make sure.

You started to breathe on your own today—for real this time! The ventilator was giving you 16 breaths per minute, but you were breathing 24/min. This means that you were taking 8 breaths/min. on your own! This is fantastic! As you can tolerate it, they will continue to reduce the number of breaths that they give you and let you do more on your own. It is a gradual process, and you are working very hard. In a couple of days, there is no telling how good you will be doing!

They took you off of the continuous dialysis today and put you on an intermittent machine. This will not be working all the time—3-4 hours a day at the most. This is a sign that your blood work is good, since you don't need to be continuously cleaned out. One step at a time...

Stayed overnight Saturday: Aunt Anne and Sharon

Sunday, December 31, 2000

You did good overnight. Aunt Anne and Sharon said that earlier in the evening, it was obvious that you had a fever—you were warm and flushed. But, somehow your fever broke before morning. The nurses didn't give you anything to control the fever—you did it yourself. They said you felt a lot better and looked better in the morning, so you did a good job of controlling whatever the problem was.

They put you on the intermittent dialysis today and cleaned out your catheter. In three hours, they took 3 liters of fluid off of you—that is 7 pounds of water! When I told you that you lost 7 pounds in 3 hours, you opened your eyes! I knew you just wanted to say, "Yes!" You gave me something to smile about! ☺

They put you back on a little insulin. You were never taken off of it completely—they put you on a "sliding scale." The nurses say it is common after this kind of trauma and the large amount of sedation you are on that some organs will slow down, and your pancreas is no exception. So, the only drips you are on are: Fentanyl (100 mg/hr), insulin (8 units/hr) and saline (15 cc/hr simply to keep your vein open). The room looks a lot bigger now that there is only one blue port—instead of <u>nine</u>!

At 6:00 p.m., you felt hot and I just knew you were getting another fever. I called the nurse in, and you were at 39.4°C. They gave you a bath to help cool you down. When I told you goodnight, you opened your eyes. We know you can't see, but it is encouraging to see pupils! ☺

Stayed overnight: Missy and Roddy

Monday, January 1, 2001

Guess what—you have an infection! Big surprise, considering your fever. This one is different, though, because it (the bacteria) has moved from your lung to your bloodstream. The doctor told Dad that the only way the bacteria could leave your lungs is if it chewed a hole through them. The bacteria is *Pseudomonas*—the same one you had last week. Go figure! This can cause pneumonia, but they don't think you have that yet. You are still getting daily chest x-rays, and your lungs are looking better than they did before, but they still don't look good. I told the nurse that you were a smoker and that your lungs might not have been perfect <u>before</u> the accident, and she said that smoking could delay the healing process since the junk in your lungs could hold on to bugs. But, your day nurse is very optimistic that you will kick this infection in a few days.

Needless to say, your surgery will not be tomorrow. It is tentatively scheduled for Wednesday, January 3rd. We were surprised that it wasn't postponed more than just 24 hours, but they seem to think you will be much better by then. You need to be on the dialysis machine tomorrow, as I said a few days ago, and they have to give you heparin when you are on it. The orthopedic surgeons decided not to cut on you when you are on blood thinners—go figure—so they put the surgery off for a day. Hopefully, by Wednesday, this infection will be under control and the surgery will go off without a hitch. You will stay on antibiotics for probably 14 days to make sure everything dies this time, but the staff thinks that you and the drugs will take care of the infection in the next few days.

At 6:00 p.m., your temperature had gone down to 100.6°F—you were at 103°F a few hours before. The Tylenol is working! Your glucose levels are getting really high now though. You just got 25 units of insulin and then they had to give you some more through your central line. Your nurse says that your high glucose proves that your body is fighting the infection, but she left before I could figure out the details. I will ask the next nurse later.

So, the next nurse was useless. She couldn't answer any of my questions and she told me to only look at the "big picture" and not pay attention to details that we can't understand. I know that I know more about your situation that she does, and she talks to me like I'm a little kid. We aren't friends! I have no new information from her. A doctor came in to talk to me around 11:30 p.m. Val hinted to the nurse that we would like to talk to a doctor, if possible. I got to ask her some questions, and then she told me that she wouldn't have time to do this every night. No problem—I won't ask her shit again! All I know is that your fever went down some, and that might or might not indicate that you are getting the infection under control. What kind of an answer is that? Nice explanation. So, I have to wait until tomorrow to get a new nurse who knows something and get to talk to a different doctor before I can figure out what's going on with you.

On top of everything else, you have a yeast infection! They are giving you some medicine for it and putting stuff in your mouth to make sure it doesn't grow there. Hopefully, that will get cleared up soon and the idiot nurse and rude doctor can go away! ☺

Stayed overnight Monday: Theresa, Corey and Valerie

Tuesday, January 2, 2001

This morning, I got to come in around 6:30 a.m. You did not feel hot anymore, so I'm guessing your fever went (or stayed) down. You had the same nurse and doctor and I didn't feel like getting aggravated again, so I didn't ask what they did overnight. I will wait until after rounds.

You are in isolation—which just means that we have to wear a gown and gloves so we don't carry the *Pseudomonas* bacteria to any other patients.

This morning when I was in there, they didn't kick me out at 7:00 a.m. like usual—I think they thought I was part of the staff. Since I got to stay longer, I was able to brush your hair. Your nurse had started it, but she said she didn't have time to finish it. You lost a lot of hair when I combed it because of all of the rats. It took them so long to wash it because your head was very delicate in the beginning, so the blood and glass in your hair tangled it up. I couldn't brush out the back, but I got the sides as good as possible. I am going to ask Debbie to bring scissors the next time she comes over to trim you up—your ends are damaged from being tangled for so long. Your hair needed to be combed out because they were going to continue to get worse and we don't want nurses to cut your hair off. Before I came in the room, your mean arterial blood pressure was 59. The rude doctor from last night was calling your name and messing with you and your BP did not change and you did not respond. When I started talking, your BP went up in the high 60s and when I brushed your hair and talked, it jumped up to the high 70s! I know you can recognize my voice. You are responding very well to familiar voices! It's just a matter of time before you're looking at us and talking to us.

You were on dialysis today from 8:30 a.m. to 12:00 p.m. They pulled off 5 liters of fluid in that 3 ½ hours—that is over 10 pounds of juice. They were encouraged that you held your BP up high enough for them to pull off all of the fluid. Your heart appears to be doing well! I think I mentioned in here before that the head doctor wanted to get as much fluid out of you as possible, while putting minimal amounts in, and keep your BP up—and you appear to be doing that! The next big step is, of course, the hip surgery and the ventilator/feeding tubes getting removed from your mouth. As soon as we can talk to a doctor, which seems to be more difficult than it sounds, we can figure out how you are fighting the bacteria infection. It looks like the surgery is still set for tomorrow, so you must be a little better.

We didn't get to talk to a doctor all day. For some reason, your day nurse was just as stupid as your night nurse. She didn't want to figure out how you were handling your infection because she figured that the doctors would talk to us as a group. She was just lazy and really annoying.

I happened to be visiting you when the doctors made their evening rounds around 5:30 p.m. I heard them say that the surgery was still on the schedule and your bacteria infection wasn't even mentioned—so I guess it's under control. Who knows?!

The last thing we heard tonight was that the surgery and operating room were scheduled for 8:30 a.m. to 12:30 p.m. tomorrow (Wednesday). Your fever is (or appears to be) gone and you are breathing easily. You look good and appear to be stable since they think you can handle an intense surgery. We'll find out tomorrow!

Stayed overnight Tuesday: Uncle Tom

Wednesday, January 3, 2001

You were wheeled to the operating room at 8:45 a.m. with your eyes wide open. Dad and Uncle Tom got to see you before you left and they thought you looked good and ready to go! They didn't expect to hear anything until 2:00 p.m.

At 2:30 p.m., an orthopedic surgeon came in to tell us that your hip was fixed! They were very pleased with how well the surgery went. The head hip doctor had told this doctor that you would hardly be able to tell that your hip was fractured once it healed. The break wasn't as hard to fix as they originally thought and waiting 20 days before surgery didn't cause huge problems. Unfortunately, the trachea and feeding tubes were not put in. The orthopedic surgeon said that you had a slight blood oxygenation problem, and they didn't think you were stable enough to handle it. So, you were brought back to the ICU at 3:00 p.m. and we had to wait to talk to a general surgeon or an ICU doctor to tell us what the problem was. Since it had been so hard the past 48 hours to get a doctor to talk to us, Dad went into ICU and raised ten types of hell. Within 30 minutes, we were all in a conference room with the ICU fellow. He didn't tell us anything exciting—just that your oxygen saturation percentages dropped to the low 90s and they wanted you to be breathing better before they messed with you. They moved you to a bigger room to make it more "dialysis accessible," so you went from Room 8 to Room 17.

You were part of a research study at around 4:30 p.m. The nurse who suggested this study on December 18th came in and asked if we had discussed whether or not to allow you to be in the study. It would evaluate how your brain responds to visual and audio stimuli while under sedation. We thought it would be a good idea since, if for no other reason, we would get to know how your brain was working. A few of us got to watch while they did the tests. Dad said that you obviously responded, according to the nurse, and you also remembered the stimuli afterwards. Even though these are preliminary exams, we are very encouraged. We know that you are in there, and we just need to wait for you to wake up! ☺

You looked great after surgery and made it through a difficult day wonderfully. We can't wait to see how you are tomorrow!

By the way, your Oklahoma Sooners won the NCAA Football National Championship tonight! We knew you would love that!

Stayed overnight Wednesday: Uncle Phil and Aunt Debbie

Thursday, January 4, 2001

You had some trouble keeping your blood pressure up overnight. Our favorite nurse said they were going to give you blood to help you out. By the time you went on dialysis at 11:00 a.m., your pressure had stabilized. They want to take 4 liters of fluid off of you and give you two units of blood.

You still have a bacteria infection. It appears that you are resistant to the antibiotics they were giving you, so you are getting a new one. This should hopefully take care of it. It would be a lot easier on you if this bacteria would go away. You aren't spiking high fevers, and that is a good sign that you are doing better. If we could ever talk to someone who knows anything, I could tell you more.

At 4:00 p.m. while I was in your room, I finally met the doctor who will be taking care of you everyday. She is fantastic! She came in and told us everything about you! They are narrowing their focus as to what injuries you have "left." As far as your infection, she thinks that the antibiotics you are on are working and it should be cleared soon. Since it is in your blood, there is always a chance that it could spread to other organs or to your bones—which would be awful. But she doesn't think that is going to happen. In fact, the problem that they want to address immediately is removing the ventilator tube and giving you a trachea tube. This will also reduce the amount of bacteria that stays in your lungs because the ventilator hoards bugs. The doctor told Dad that she thinks you are out of the woods and within a month will be out of the ICU into a "lower" room. We also learned that you responded to the doctor before they took you to surgery yesterday. She asked you if you were in pain and you shook your head "no," and she asked if you could hear and understand her and you nodded "yes." You haven't been sober enough to respond to us, but we know that day is coming!

Just when we thought you were having an un-eventful day, you got a fever. It went up to 39.5°C (~104°F) and they re-cultured your blood to see if you picked up a new bug. You are getting Tylenol and ice bags to help control it, so we hope this one will break, too.

One piece of good news—you responded to your nurse! You were able to nod "yes" and "no" to him when he asked you questions. They are going to take you completely off the Fentanyl at 4:00 a.m. tomorrow morning. I'm not sure how long it will take you to come to, but it could take days. At any rate, you will be waking soon and we are very excited.

Stayed overnight Thursday: Theresa and Corey

Friday, January 5, 2001

So, they took you completely off the Fentanyl at 4:00 a.m. this morning. The doctors figured that by the time they went on rounds, you would be awake enough for them to evaluate your mental status. I was in your room by 3:45 a.m. to watch you wake up—I was so excited I could barely sleep. Unfortunately, things did not go as planned. Fentanyl suppressed your gag reflex apparently, and that was the first thing to come "unsuppressed." You started gagging on the multiple tubes in your mouth. By 5:30 a.m., your oxygen saturation levels dropped to 92-93% and your nurse put you back on the drugs. You never woke up or responded to commands; all that happened was that you became uncomfortable. By 7:45 a.m., you were starting to calm down, but I had to leave the room for rounds. You still had a fever and the doctor wasn't sure if you had picked up a new bacteria or if one of your cuts or entry areas (IV holes) were infected. She didn't see anything—so they will talk about what might be going on during rounds.

This afternoon, your fever broke. You looked good, but, for some reason, they didn't jump on the chance to put the trachea tube in. We don't know what the problem is. But, the orthopedic surgeons want to do something with you today. They want to give you radiation to stop any unwanted bone growth around your hip. There is medicine they could give you, but it might damage your kidneys. Considering that your kidneys aren't working as is, they didn't want to cause any further problems. You went down for the radiation therapy at 3:00 p.m. and they said you would return at 4:45 p.m. No one saw you until 8:15 p.m.! We don't know why it took so long, but you had a fever again. You were back to 25 mg of Fentanyl per hour and resting comfortably.

We still don't think that they have the blood/ lung cultures back. By tomorrow, they should know what is growing in your blood and lungs.

The antibiotics you are on now—imipenem and gentamicin—are strong and should kill anything in your system. The fever, according to the orthopedic surgeons, could simply be an after-effect of the hip surgery. The ICU doctors don't know what's happening, but they won't let you get cut on to put the trach in until you are cooled off. More waiting, but you are stable and well on your way to getting better!

Stayed overnight Friday: Uncle Dave and Aunt Anne

Saturday, January 6, 2001

We didn't know what was going on with you today until late in the afternoon. You have had a fever of 101°-103°F all day and the doctors still aren't sure what is causing it. I talked to your doctor at 9:30 p.m. and she filled me in.

You will get a CT scan of your abdomen to see if any of your organs are infected. The doctor does not expect to see anything in the CT scan, but they need to do it to rule the possibility out. Your initial CT scans didn't show them anything to indicate that you have damaged areas that bacteria could thrive in. Hopefully, nothing will show up.

The results of your blood/lung cultures came in—you are clean! No bacteria grew from either sample, so they think the infection is taken care of. You will stay on the antibiotics and continue to be in isolation for a while. It is great to hear that the infection appears to be gone.

Right now, it looks like the trach and feeding tubes will be put in on Monday morning. They don't do elective surgeries on the weekend. Unless your fever spikes again, or something funny happens, this will get taken care of on Monday. The feeding tube in your mouth will not be removed until Tuesday. They want to give the tube that will be in your stomach some time before they feed you through it to make sure there is no bleeding or any other problems.

As far as your trach tube goes, they will probably give you all day Monday to get adjusted to it and relax. By Tuesday, they are going to start messing with it. They will do things to try and see how well you can breathe on your own—this way they can start to wake you up and see what is going on in that head of yours. They are particularly worried about what damage your stroke caused—the doctor didn't mention anything about specific areas of your brain that may be damaged. They want to get you up in a chair soon, and then it won't be too long before you could leave the ICU for a "less serious" injury floor.

You seemed to be responding to your visitors very well today. Melody seemed to get your attention—imagine that! She thought your facial expressions indicated that you could hear her. Uncle Tom, Valerie, Uncle Dave and Aunt Anne also felt like you were more alert and responsive. I didn't get to mess with you very much because they wanted you to sleep, but it is obvious that you are improving every day! We can't wait to wake you up!

Sunday, January 7, 2001

Today was a pretty slow day for you. You went down for the CT scan of your abdomen at 1:00 p.m. and you were back in the ICU by 2:30 p.m. Everything looks good—there aren't any infected areas on any of your organs. They wanted to get the CT scan done today so that in case there was an infected area, it could be addressed when you are in the operating room tomorrow. Fortunately, they don't have to do anything in the OR except put the trach/feeding tubes in. We are looking forward to this!

Your fever is not going away. You have been running a temperature of 103°F all day, and Tylenol is not helping. Like I said, your blood/lung cultures aren't growing any bacteria and now the CT scan is clear, so they don't know what is causing the fever. They still aren't really concerned about it. Tomorrow at 2:00 p.m., they will take you to the OR no matter what your temperature is. If the fever is accompanied by other complications, then they will see if they need to wait. But, if everything remains as is, you will almost have a clean mouth tomorrow at 3:30 p.m.!

You are only on imipenem now—they took you off the really strong stuff. This should help you fend off any bacteria for a while. I don't think you are on any medication for the yeast infection even though you still have it. Your day nurse told me this, so I am not sure how true it is. I will find out tomorrow.

At 10:00 p.m., your temperature went down to 37.5°C! Your temp. has stayed here for around 4 hours, so I hope it is broken for good. We'll see how you do overnight!

Stayed overnight Sunday: Theresa and Valerie

Monday, January 8, 2001

You managed to keep your fever down all morning. Right before midnight, you spiked up over 39°C. They hurried to give you Tylenol before 12:00 a.m. since you couldn't get fluids after that due to the upcoming operation. Since then, you have done a good job of controlling it on your own.

The time for your surgery was moved from 2:00 p.m. to 11:30 a.m. But, an emergency surgery came in and you didn't get to go down until 1:30 p.m. Anyways, Dad got you worked up this morning! You nodded at him twice and made my heart jump! I hadn't seen you do this yet, and it was amazing! He asked you if you were blistered and you raised your eyebrows at him. It was hysterical! You followed him around with your eyes—watching him hold your hand and rub your arm. Your heart rate went up, and we knew that you recognized him!

They didn't bring you back from the operating room until 4:30 p.m. Now, you have an empty mouth! The trach and feeding tubes are in, and they want you to rest and get used to them tonight. Hopefully, you will sleep calmly overnight and be adjusted to the new tube in your throat and they can take you off the drugs!

You were really out of it at 10:00 p.m. Your eyes were wandering, but you never focused on anything. You did smile when you heard my voice. It was a closed mouth smile—you wouldn't open your mouth for anything! Your ventilator was back at its "normal" settings for you—16 breaths/minute with 40% oxygen. You just need time to rest!

Visitors: Dr. and Mrs. Bernard, me, Dad, J, Corey, Val
Calls: Kittie, Sharon

Tuesday, January 9, 2001

You were a little worked up this morning. The nurses had turned you just before 6:00 a.m. and you hate that! Your heart rate was up around 120, but you looked like you were resting well. You aren't breathing over the ventilator like you were before, but I'm sure you will once you get used to the new tube. You smiled at me again, but I couldn't get you to squeeze my hand or nod your head—maybe you will for Dad! You still don't want to open your mouth, and I don't blame you! The nurse tried to take your temperature, and you clenched your teeth and would not let her into your mouth. She had to take your temp on the side of your mouth, outside of your teeth. You still don't have a fever! It was 37.2°C. You look great!

At 11:15 a.m., you were as awake as we have ever seen you. You heard Dad's voice when he was still in the hallway, and you started smiling! He messed with you and you were smiling and trying to talk. I was at your side and Dad was playing with your toes and giving you ten types of hell and I saw you mouth the words, "f*** you." Dad had said those would be the first words you would speak when you woke up. You tried to say other things, but I couldn't read your lips any other time. We played Tina Turner and it looked like you were trying to sing along!

You got dialysis today and they pulled off 5 liters of fluid. You were a little swollen since it had been 3 days since you were last dialyzed. This morning, they drained <u>60 cc</u> of urine out of your bladder! This is three times what you made before. It is still not a whole lot, but it's a start!

Corey was holding your right hand while I did arm exercises with your left arm. I told you that your arm was going to be stronger than Corey's soon—your eyebrows raised and you gave a big smile! You got a kick out of that! You definitely recognized him—you smiled at him several times.

You had an uneventful evening. After you finished the dialysis, you were worn out and stayed asleep for the rest of the day. We were able to get you to open your eyes a little bit around 4:00 p.m., but it was nothing compared to what you did earlier. You looked very tired, so we decided to leave you alone to let you rest. Coming off the drugs will take a long time, but we are anxious to talk to you!

Calls: Uncle Bud and Aunt Laverne, Sharon, Jane
Visitors: Merle Beckemeyer (left a note)
Stayed overnight Tuesday: Uncle Tom

Wednesday, January 10, 2001

At 6:00 a.m., they drained your bladder for the first time since yesterday morning—you made 80 cc of urine in the past 24 hours! That is 20 cc more than yesterday, so you are doing a great job. They are taking you down for a CT scan of your head to see what is happening with your brain. But, that is really all you will be doing today.

You weren't very responsive today. Since you had been off the drugs for 24 hours, we figured you would be more alert than you were yesterday. Unfortunately, you weren't. You slept for most of the day, which is understandable.

At 8:00 p.m., Debbie and Phil got to go in and see you. You were finished with the CT scan, but a neurologist had not read it yet. From what your ICU doctor could see, it looked like your brain had become more bruised. We are not sure what part of your brain they are worried about—we think it is your cerebellum where the stroke occurred. At 9:00 p.m., the neurologists called the ICU and asked if your CT scan had to be addressed tonight—was it a life or death emergency—and the ICU doctor told them "no." As far we know, you will get a neurology consult first thing Thursday morning. Then, we will know for sure what the CT scan showed.

Tonight, the ICU doctors were concerned about the fact that you haven't regained consciousness and are not moving around yet. They are afraid that you might never wake up. This definitely shocked us, considering how great you were responding yesterday. When we went to bed, we weren't sure if they thought you were going to be in a vegetative state or a coma or what. It was very scary. I think you just need more time, and we will wait patiently.

Stayed overnight Wednesday: Uncle Phil and Aunt Debbie
Visitors: Orland and Linda, Charlie and Candy, Connie and Ashley

Thursday, January 11, 2001

This morning you were more awake than yesterday. Phil and Debbie said you were smiling and had your eyes open again! This was encouraging since all we got was bad news last night. At 6:00

a.m., they drained your bladder and you made 150 cc of urine in the past 24 hours! This is fantastic news! That is 70 cc more than the previous 24 hour period. It still isn't a lot, but you are definitely moving in the right direction!

At 12:00 p.m., Corey, Veronica and I got your attention. You were smiling and swallowing and had your eyes open. It is so good to see you awake! One of the best nurses in this unit took care of you last night. She told Phil and Debbie that you had been getting so much Fentanyl for so long that it is probably stored up in your fat cells. Because of this, it will take a long time to get it out of your system, especially since your kidneys aren't working like they normally do and you are only getting dialysis every other day. I can tell that you are in there—you just need some more time.

A neurologist and two of his residents came in to check you out around 3:30 p.m. They played around with you for a few minutes—I didn't get to see them do a whole lot of examining. Afterwards, they talked to me in the hallway outside of your room. They told me that the reason that you had the CT scan yesterday was to see if you sustained any brain damage when you came down with rhabdomyolysis. That night (Friday, 12/22/00), your mean arterial blood pressure ranged from 40-70 mmHg. You needed to keep it above 60 to make sure your brain was thoroughly perfused. Since it went below 60 for probably long periods of time, they thought brain damage was possible. The neurologists didn't say too much about what the CT scan showed, but they were concerned with the fact that you haven't moved the rest of your body. The doctors said that this could be due to a couple of things:

Result of rhabdomyolysis—so much of your muscle degraded that you cannot move your limbs

Myosin deficiency—our bodies require actin and myosin to work together to get our muscles to contract. It is common for people who have been laying down and not moving for a while to have a deficiency in myosin, making it near impossible to get muscle contraction.

They are also going to do an EEG on your brain tomorrow and just see what is going on. You could have any number of abnormalities in your brain function, and many can be corrected with medicine. For instance, you could be having seizures, but, since you can't move your body, we wouldn't be able to tell without this test. Seizures can be treated with drugs. Some problems are untreatable, and we desperately hope that, if you have any problems, they will not fall into this category.

They also want to run a few tests on your muscles: EMG, muscle biopsy and ulnar nerve stimulation. The EMG and ulnar nerve test will evaluate how your nervous system is transmitting signals—whether or not the synapses between neurons are in good shape. I don't know for sure what the muscle biopsy is for, but I will find out tomorrow. All of these tests should be completed by 4:00 p.m. Friday, and we will have a much better idea of the kind of shape your brain is in.

You got dialyzed today. They only took off three liters of fluid, so it didn't wear you out that much. I don't know what they look at to determine how much fluid to draw out of you, but I will find out.

You were pretty responsive today. Jessica told you to wake up because there were good-looking men all over the place, and you smiled at her! You also smiled when you saw Veronica! It had been a while since you had seen her. You responded to other comments, too! We had fun with you!

Friday, January 12, 2001

You had a good morning. No fever, no changes. They only drained 80 cc of urine out of your bladder today. I hope you can make more tomorrow!

The neurology team did the EEG at 9:00 a.m. The head neurologist said that he saw no abnormalities, except that it looked slower than normal. He said that this could be caused by a list of things that have nothing to do with your brain function, so it being slow doesn't really indicate anything. But, it is great that there isn't anything wrong that they could see. When they tested your ulnar nerve, however, you did not respond. This could be due to a nerve problem or a muscle problem—they don't know which, or even if something else could be inhibiting your movement. They plan to do a muscle biopsy, which will detect any muscle abnormalities, and an EMG (I don't know what it stands for yet), which will detect any nerve abnormalities. When these results get in, they will have a different picture of what is going on.

Your nurse said the drug you were on and the large dosages that you were given could be the reason that you aren't moving yet. I will do a little research on fentanyl and see what exactly this drug can do. If the fentanyl is causing you to not move, then it is temporary! I will learn more about the drug and fill you in later.

You were responsive again today. I talked to you for almost three hours, and you became more alert as time went by. I told you why you were in the hospital and what all had happened. Afterwards, I asked you if you understood and you nodded. John Gheradini came in, and you recognized him. I told you that you were going to be okay, and you smiled. I asked if you trusted me, and you nodded! I have a great feeling that you are going to recover from this and get back to your old self—I was happy to know that you believed me!

You went down to Interventional Radiology around 2:45 p.m. They wanted to remove the central line from the right side of your neck, and put it where you are currently hooked up for dialysis. Now, there will be three openings in the same spot on your neck. When you came back to the ICU at 5:00 p.m., you were passed out. Road trips often make you tired, so this wasn't any different than normal. Corey, Jessica and I thought about waking you up, but you looked exhausted, so we left you alone. I got to talk to some doctors, but they didn't have any new news. Maybe tomorrow.

Visitors: John, Corey, Jessica and Theresa

Saturday, January 13, 2001

I called the ICU at 9:30 a.m. to see how you were doing, and you had a nurse that I think is stupid. You had her last week and she <u>really</u> got on my nerves. She is useless! She did tell me that you only made 60 cc of urine, your temperature is 37.9°C, and you will get dialysis today. I will call again around 8:30 p.m. when I know she is gone.

You had a better nurse this evening. There were no problems throughout the day. They took 4 liters off of you with dialysis today and you tolerated it pretty well. You were about the same as before in terms of alertness. You were making facial expressions and mouthing words—you were even looking at the TV! Today was a good rest day!

Sunday, January 14, 2001

Today was another rest day for you. They drained 90 cc of urine out of your bladder this morning! You did well overnight—but you got another fever. It was only around 102°, but they cultured you again to see what was happening. Hopefully, it's nothing.

Uncle Tom and Uncle Steve came to see you on their way home from retreat. Uncle Tom apparently got you going! The nurses and our favorite ICU doctor got a big kick out of that!

Your fever broke this evening. No problem! They turned your ventilator down to only give you 8 breaths per minute and you were doing anywhere from 10 to 16 breaths per minute on your own! This is very exciting! You are doing so well. We are looking forward to the muscle biopsy and EMG. You are also going to get an MRI of your head and neck to compare with the CT scan.

Other than this, you relaxed all day!

Visitors: Uncle Tom and Uncle Steve

Monday, January 15, 2001

You were comfortable overnight—no more fever or mentionable problems. You made 75 cc of urine in the past 24 hours, which is still hardly anything. However, the ICU doctor told Dad that there are signs that your kidneys are working better. In between dialysis sessions, levels of certain things (I don't know what) tend to increase simply because they are storing up. In your case, they have not been increasing between dialysis sessions, indicating that your kidneys are doing something.

Great news! You will get dialysis again tomorrow to help clean you out.

They came in to do the muscle biopsy this afternoon. I don't know how long it will take to get the results—hopefully not too long.

You got the MRI of your head and neck tonight—we should know something by tomorrow night. Today was a quiet day!

Grandma, Uncle Dave and Aunt Anne visited with you for a few hours. You weren't very responsive, but you did smile for Grandma! We all know that your recovery is going to be slow, but everyone hopes that you will just sit up and get back to normal. It is going to take some time to get you totally off the fentanyl, since there was so much stored in your body. Everyone just needs to be more patient.

By tomorrow, we should know a little bit more about the condition of your body and brain. I hope that you just need physical therapy to build your muscles up to get you to move again, and you just need to get the drugs out of your system to be more awake. The tests will tell us, but this is my gut feeling. I know you are in there! I can't wait to talk to you! Jessica, Dad and I got a rise out of you a few times, but we are ready for you to be fully awake.

Visitors: Grandma, Uncle Dave, Aunt Anne, Jessica, Tony and Theresa

Tuesday, January 16, 2001

Today was great! First of all, you made 120 cc of urine since yesterday! Back on the upward swing! Second, you were more alert than I have seen you yet! You were mouthing words all day. You said, "how's your arm?" to Corey and you said, "where's your Dad?" to me. It was a lot of fun to talk to you because you were so alert and responsive.

We waited to hear the results of your MRI, but no one knew what it showed. The ICU doctor said that it would take a while because it had to go through radiology, neurology, ICU and then we could hear something. Unfortunately, the ICU doctors still didn't know what was going on.

Dad, Corey and I left around 3:30 p.m. You were very exhausted, and we knew you needed to rest. You had dialysis today. They tried to take three liters of fluid off of you, but you didn't tolerate it very well. Your blood pressure kept dropping, so the dialysis nurse kept giving you fluid. Overall, whatever they took out, they put back in. This was the first time, that I can remember, that you didn't tolerate fluid removal. Usually, you deal with it pretty well.

This evening, the head attending ICU doctor called Dad. He said that 90% of the MRI had been read, but he didn't want to comment until it had been completely interpreted. He wants us to be at the hospital tomorrow so we could talk to all of the teams that are working with you at once. So, that can't be good news. Otherwise, he probably would have at least given Dad a little bit of positive feedback. How can you only read 90% of an MRI? You either read it or you don't. But, either way, we won't find out until tomorrow. I guess they are going to let us know how your brain looks and what they want to do next. They did another EEG tonight—I'm not sure why—but, they'll tell us about it tomorrow. The results of the muscle biopsy will not be available until next week, but they can clue us in without knowing what that says. Tomorrow is a <u>BIG</u> day!

Visitors: Corey, Tony and Theresa

Wednesday, January 17, 2001

Today was awful. You were sleeping for most of the day, so you obviously didn't respond much. We got a huge bomb dropped on us at 2:15 p.m.—we learned what the MRI showed. It turns out that, at some point, blood did not sufficiently perfuse your cervical spinal cord. This means that you had a stroke in your neck area, and that part of you is damaged. Because of this, you will never be able to move from the neck down. In addition, there is evidence of bleeding in the middle of your brain. I don't know how, but this makes it damn near impossible for you to ever get any better, or more awake, than you are right now. You will never get back to the old Aunt Ruth—that part of you is gone. So, basically, we are left with two options:

1) We could either continue with the treatment you are currently receiving and place you in a long-term care facility for the rest of your life, which would most likely be very short—with the blood infections and your need for dialysis, the doctors feel like you have a number of things that could make you very sick once you left the ICU

2) We could stop the dialysis and/or ventilator and/or feeding tube and let you die peacefully

The way you are now is the way you will be forever with the only possible improvements being miniscule, if any. This was not what I expected to hear. I have felt for so long that you were going to wake up soon, and having that conversation was devastating. We just can't believe it. I just wanted to collapse walking out of the conference room. I had been praying that you would just wake up and everything could get back to normal. I had no idea how bad off you were. I thought we made it out of the woods. Now, it seems almost unfair to you to keep fighting to keep you alive.

When I went back to your room, it just wasn't the same. Knowing that you aren't just going to sit up and start talking like the old you—your body really is just a shell. Why keep the shell here if there is no Aunt Ruth to fill it? This really blows me away. Today just sucked.

We all went to Centralia. Dad wanted to talk to Grandma and give her all of the details before anyone outside of the family called her. Corey, Jessica and I just didn't want to be in Collinsville. Your Christmas presents from me and J were in the living room and I lost it when I saw them. I just wish things could be different. I wish this never would have happened. I can't put into words how much I am going to miss you. You are so important to me and so many others.

This is so hard for Dad. He is heartbroken. We'll see what happens tomorrow. I'm too upset to write anymore today...

Thursday, January 18, 2001

No decisions had been made, as far as I knew, by this morning. I didn't get there until noon and I could only stay until 1:00 p.m. because I had to take off for an interview, so I didn't get to find out much. I think all of your brothers and Aunt Jeannie and Grandma are deciding what you would want them to do in this situation. I'm sure they all feel the same way.

You were kind of responsive. You were able to smile and nod. I gave you some water with a green swab and you loved it. I scrubbed your teeth and lips and you would bite down on the sponge to get all of the water out. Melody and I decided that tomorrow I should give you some Walker's Deluxe instead of water! If she brings the flask—consider it done! When I left, I told you that I loved you and that I would see you tomorrow and you nodded. I also asked if you would go with me to my St. Louis University interview and you nodded. No words today—you were too tired. I wish I could have gotten the interview invitation before the accident—you would have loved that! You would know more doctors at SLU than I ever would!!

There was a problem with dialysis today. The nurses couldn't get the machine to work because you have apparently clotted off the catheter opening. The only way that a new one could be put in is if you went down to Interventional Radiology and they went through the whole procedure to replace it. No one wants to put you through that, and I don't know what the next step will be.

So, you may not have to get dialysis anymore. We'll see what Dad has to say. He will do the best thing for you.

Fun things you did today:

~Melody was talking about taking the emerald, and I asked if I could have the 10 carat, and you nodded!! ☺

~You smiled when we said we would give you Walker's tomorrow!

~Melody said she was going to put Corey in the bed with you because he hit his head and you smiled!

~I kissed your head and told you that I loved you—I hope not for the last time.

Friday, January 19, 2001

You were alert this morning—smiling and nodding. Dad went in to talk to you to see what you understood. He asked you if you were ready to go to sleep and see Doc, and you nodded and smiled! He realized that you understood that things weren't going to get any better and you wanted to rest. He knew it was okay. Everyone decided last night that letting you go was the best thing. Knowing that you will never get back to the way you were—it's not fair to want to keep you here.

The doctors called your brothers into the infamous conference room that we've been given bad news in before. They explained how they were going to take you off the ventilator. The doctors would give you a large dose of fentanyl to help you relax and not fight. They would unplug the ventilator and let you breathe on your own. You will definitely not get dialysis again. Having no dialysis for 4 days will help you to pass on soon.

The ventilator was taken off at around 2:00 p.m. You did pretty well on your own. By 6:30 p.m., when I got to the hospital from the airport, you were taking one breath every eight seconds. This was just enough to keep your oxygen saturation levels in the 80s. You looked very strong. It was pretty obvious that your body was fixed—outside of the broken bones. You've really come a long way since the accident.

You didn't change much overnight. Your numbers stayed solid. I knew it would only be a matter of time before the high potassium messed with your heart. I went home to take my dress shoes off ☺ and get some rest, and I hoped I would see you on Saturday.

Saturday, January 20, 2001

Well, today is Melody's birthday! We could not believe that you could possibly die on the same day that Doc delivered #8! Melody is so excited that the two of you can share this day. I told her that you did this so that no one in our family will forget her birthday. She said that this was your way of leaving her a family!

You were breathing steady and going strong all day.

You had a lot of visitors: Grandma, Tim, Steve and Jeannie, Mom and Dad, Steve and Linda, me, Corey, Jessica, Valerie, Vern, Missy, Melody and Ashley and John Gheradini. Dave & Anne and Debbie & Phil were here yesterday. Uncle Phil had chest pain and went to the ER at St. Mary's—he found out that he pulled a muscle in his neck. No heart problems, thank God!

You barely changed at all until around 6:30 p.m. Your nurse was giving you some Versed to help you relax. At the same time, you apparently had a heart attack. Your heart rate dropped from 98 to 65 immediately, and your oxygen saturation levels went from 70% down to the 30s. I got really scared and called Dad—he had walked downstairs with Tim. But you stabilized—relatively speaking, of course. The shape of the heart beats on the computer changed. They were totally different than before—it went from ⁓⁓⁓ to ⁓⁓⁓ . The nurse thought that this change was indicative of a heart attack. You were able to get back to a regular rhythm. Your oxygen saturation levels got back into the 60s-70s and your blood pressure was higher than right after the heart attack—your mean BP got down to 38 and afterwards it was in the 50s.

You stayed this way until around 9:00 p.m. Then, you started having an irregular heartbeat and alarms started going off because of all of the missed heartbeats. At 9:20 p.m., Dad and Tim walked around the hallway. I sat down by you and told you that I wasn't going to get excited unless your heart rate dropped below 40 because you had been in the low 40s for a while. As soon as I said that, your heart rate went to 39 then 35 and I got nervous. I asked Melody if I should call Dad, and your heart rate jumped into the 60s! Melody told me that we have to leave Dad out of this or you will never die! ☺

Right then, I saw Dad's shadow behind the curtain and I relaxed immediately. He came to the bed, grabbed your hand and said, "Ruthie, here's the deal…" and you flatlined. It was unbelievable! It was like you waited to know he was there and then let go. We all kind of gasped because we had been watching you for so long—it was kind of amazing when you passed away.

It was such a great feeling to know that you were in a better place. Where you are now is so much better than this ICU room!

Melody had placed a rose from the arrangement that Joe had sent her for her birthday on your chest. When you passed way, you really looked the same as you had during the previous 24 hours. Your color hardly changed, which was very surprising. You looked beautiful, and we were all relieved. None of us wanted you to be in pain any longer. We were all in such a peaceful mood because your suffering was over. We knew you were with Doc and you were happier than you had been in a long time.

We cleaned the personal stuff out of your room, called everybody and said goodbye to the ICU staff. Our favorite ICU doctor was the one who came in your room to make sure your heart had stopped. You passed away at 9:26 p.m. We decided that you had a 9:30 dinner date with Doc. You hadn't had a cocktail in 5 ½ weeks and we knew you were ready for one! We are going to miss you so much.

Your funeral was Wednesday, January 24, 2001. The Church was absolutely packed! You had tons of flowers! Fr. Doughtery gave a wonderful homily. Everybody's favorite nurse came to the service! Dad was so impressed. We all decided that he was nuts about you!

Your nephews were pall bearers and your nieces brought up the gifts. Everyone went to Calvary after the Mass. It looked like "Field of Dreams" with all of the cars lined up with their lights on. It was awesome!

Fr. Darin said a prayer and we left after 30 minutes. I took a yellow rose from your casket bouquet. We went back to St. Mary's for lunch ☺ and then I think the entire family took a nap.

I will miss you so much. I love you more than you will ever know.

Until I see you again...

I will never forget watching my Aunt Ruth die. I can remember being so thankful when she passed and relieved to know that her suffering was over. Everything was going to be okay, and I was so happy to leave the ICU knowing that I would not be coming back the next day. It was a very peaceful ending to a confusing and unstable thirty-seven days.

The realization that she was actually gone didn't come until the next night. Lots of friends and family came over to my parents' house to visit and pay their respects. I thought I was comfortable with her death. I thought I had started the grieving process days before. The worst was over, right? Not even close.

The funeral was extremely difficult, as I had expected. I was in good shape until I heard the church bells as we walked through the parking lot. They sounded so ominous, so final. It was the first time in 22 years of hearing those same bells that I was afraid to walk into the Church. I knew how bad it was going to hurt.

The whole time Aunt Ruth was in the hospital, I tried to stay optimistic. I wasn't going to give up on her. I spent so much time learning about her injuries, reading about her illnesses, and asking endless questions to anyone who looked like a nurse or a doctor. But, at the funeral, I realized that there was nothing else that could be done—no more operations, no more CT scans, no more lab results, no more medications, no more doctors. It was over. It was all over. It just took a few days to fully sink in that she was gone and there was nothing that anybody could do about it. For weeks, I had been occupying my mind with all of the details of her injuries. At the funeral, when there was nothing else to think about, I felt amazingly helpless. Everything was out of my control. But, then again, someone else had been in control the entire time. I had just been too busy to realize it.

My family has a very positive attitude towards death. We believe without a doubt that there is a heaven, and we will all be reunited in the end. These beliefs made Aunt Ruth's death easier to accept, easier to swallow. Death isn't necessarily a "bad" thing—it definitely wasn't in Aunt Ruth's case. This understanding has become a part of my professional life, as well. There were a number of occasions during my third and fourth years of medical school when I asked my residents, "do we think this patient is really going to make it through?" or "does the family understand how sick this patient is?" As I think about these things for my own patients, I always go back to Aunt Ruth's hospitalization. What did I want to know? How did I want people to talk to me? How scared was I? It made taking care of my patients much easier because I felt like I had been in their shoes.

It's not uncommon for the medical student to spend the most time with the patients. Medical students have the most time and the least responsibility. Compared to the residents, who may see around 6-8 patients every morning, the medical student can take longer talking to and examining his/her 1-2 patients before rounds. Because of this, medical students can learn more about family dynamics and what questions or concerns the patient may have. I was never afraid to talk with patients or their families because I knew they needed someone to explain what a test meant or what a medication could fix. I had no problem with that because I remembered the confusion, the uncertainty. I could take their concerns to the rest of the doctors taking care of these patients. If I couldn't answer their questions, there was always someone that could. It was just a matter of taking the time to find out what their questions were. I can't say for certain that I would have been so understanding of their needs had I not gone through this experience with my Aunt Ruth.

Now, as I begin my residency in general surgery, I am hoping that I always remember what it was like to be a family member of a patient. In many ways, I know that this understanding will make me a better doctor. Though I will not have personal knowledge of every situation, just understanding how it feels to be on the other side of the fence should serve my patients well.

The course of a hospitalization can change instantaneously. One moment, you feel as if you have a handle on the situation and things are moving in a positive direction. The next, you have been bombarded with devastating news and you are unsure of what the day will bring. While there is no way to change the uncertainty a patient and family experience, the key to minimizing the confusion is communication. Frequent conversations between members of the health care staff and the patient and family members is essential. This not only helps keep everyone informed about treatment plans, but it also makes the patient feel as if his/her needs are being met. Taking care of the whole patient, not just treating broken bones or abnormal test results, is a balancing act. In some ways, the medical staff needs to stay separated from the situation emotionally in order to do what is best for the health of the patient. However, it is impossible to truly understand what is of the most benefit to a patient if you are not aware of their life circumstances.

Some people want to know everything possible—every detail, every test result, every new discussion during rounds. Whereas other people only care to know the big things—when significant changes to the overall treatment plan are being put into place. It is up to both parties—the patient and the health care staff—to make sure that all communication lines are open. As is very obvious in my journal, I wanted to know everything that was going on with Aunt Ruth. Even the smallest positive finding made me feel better—helped me to have the strength to get up the next morning and remain optimistic. Looking back now, I got extremely excited about physical findings or lab results that really didn't change anything about her condition or her prognosis. But, it was all I had. It may not have seemed like much to the nurses or doctors, but the little things were what got me through each day. Had I not asked dozens of questions every time a nurse or doctor came near Aunt Ruth's room, I wouldn't have known as much as I did about her condition. So, my advice to anyone in a similar situation, if there is something you want to know—ASK! Don't be afraid to become involved. There are many sick people in the hospital and the staff can get busy. The only way to make sure you have the most up-to-date information is to make someone take the time to give it to you. For the most part, any member of the health care staff would be more than happy to explain points of confusion. They are generally excited to share their knowledge with people who are interested. Just let them know that you need their assistance in understanding the situation. Hopefully, they will take care of the rest.

The most important piece of advice I have to offer to patients and family members is to never give up hope. When someone you love gets sick, the illness can consume you. It becomes difficult to concentrate on anything else. It can be very easy to give in—to start to give up hope. Sometimes, the ups and downs of an illness can become so frustrating that giving in seems more logical than hanging on. However, I don't regret one moment of wishful thinking. It got me through the bad days, which is sometimes all you can ask for. I knew when the outlook was bad. I knew when a test result was severely abnormal. I knew when she wasn't responding appropriately that there was something horribly wrong. But, I had to believe that she was going to get better. So, instead of giving up hope, I decided to wait until a doctor told me to believe otherwise. The staff will let you know when nothing else can be done, and those words cut like a knife no matter how well you have been preparing yourself. If the prognosis is still in the works, stay positive! Take time with your loved ones and stay in an optimistic mood. The pain of losing someone you love is intense—don't let it grab a hold of you too soon.

The pain is real. The pain can be unbearable. There is no prayer or blessing or condolence that can make some situations easier to handle. However, telling myself that she is in a better place—out of her suffering and in the hands of God—made her death more of a positive experience. Situations like this can be too much to deal with alone. Regardless of your religion, find a higher power to share your burden with. Realize that you can't control the chaos around you and try to cherish the fact that your faith will get you through. When the pain and grief hit you, pray that you can have the strength to handle it. Just try to remember that, like all things, this too shall pass.

Everyone who knew Aunt Ruth misses her. There are always times that you just wish she was around. We all tell stories, we all tell jokes—we are probably the only group of people that can laugh and kid around while our hearts are breaking. But, that's what she would have wanted. She could have a good time anywhere, and it's important that we carry on her tradition.

I think we all take ourselves and the grind of daily life a little less seriously now. We understand that life, as we know it, can dramatically change at any given time. You should enjoy what time you have and the people you love because you never know what tomorrow will bring. Family, which was always a top priority for the Schwartz's, became something we all cherished and appreciated like we never had before. The things that seemed so important before the accident—school, work, money—didn't really seem to matter. Family and friends are ultimately what make you happy. Now, more than ever, we all truly believe this concept.

About The Author

Theresa Schwartz, M.D. grew up in Centralia, Illinois amidst apple orchards and oil fields. She graduated from St. Louis University School of Medicine and is a resident in General Surgery at St. Louis University Hospital in St. Louis, MO.